Nazam Ganj

Nazam Ganj

Worldwide Published by

Pendown Press

PENDOWN PRESS

An ISO 9001 & ISO 14001 Certified Co.,

Regd. Office: 2525/193, 1st Floor, Onkar Nagar-A,
Tri Nagar, Delhi-110035
Ph.: 09350849407, 09312235086
E-mail: info@pendownpress.com
Branch Office: 1A/2A, 20, Hari Sadan, Ansari Road,
Daryaganj, New Delhi-110002
Ph.: 011-45794768
Website: PendownPress.com

First Edition: 2021
Second Edition: 2023

ISBN: 978-93-90479-30-6

Layout and Cover Designed by Pendown Graphics Team
Printed and Bound in India by Thomson Press India Ltd.

CONTENTS

Sweta Rai

ज़ंजीरें	1
शब्दों का पिंजरा	3
मेरी ज़िंदगी, मेरा ख्वाब	5
देश रंगीला	6
देश प्रेम	7

Sneha Abhishek

Plight	11
मैंने जीना सीख लिया	13
Happy Birthday Darling	15
तुम नारी हो, बराबरी क्यों करती हो?	17

Richa Srivastava

समय	21
Yolo	23
Pronouns	26

Bipasha Bharti

Feeling lonely	31
सखी	33
मौसम	36

ABOUT THE AUTHOR

Sweta Rai, a student of education field in Delhi University, did schooling from a convent school in Noida. While doing her bachelor's she read theories of many philosophers and started observing society very closely. It enabled her to think critically, and then to represent her thoughts into words she started writing. Since then she has a passion for writing and tries to reflect on various social issues through poems to reach to a wider public. Her writings are also greatly influenced by her experience as a girl from a middle class family in a metropolitan city. Her Poems are musical reality, they are music to ears and at the same time shows the present reality of the society and compels to think more. It's her first book as an author.

"Everything around us is a poem; we just need to find appropriate words to describe it."

She would like to thank **Akshita** for providing illustrations.

–Sweta Rai

ज़ंजीरें

अभी तो टूटी हैं जंजीरें पैरों से,
थोड़ा उनका घाव तो भरने दो।

अकड़न है पैरों में अभी, थोड़ा उनको भी,
दो गज से आगे चलने की आदत तो डलने दो।

अभी तो शुरू किया है,
थोड़ा गिर कर खुद से तो संभलने दो।

क्या सही क्या नहीं,
जानने के लिए थोड़ी गलतियाँ तो करने दो।

उन गलतियों को मेरी काबिलियत का प्रश्नचिह्न बनाकर,
दोबारा मेरे पैरों को चार दीवारी के खूंटे में मत बंधने दो।

अभी तो रोशनी का लुफ्त लेना शुरू किया है,
फिर दोबारा उस अंधेरे के कुएँ में मत गिरने दो।

अभी तो टूटी हैं जंजीरें पैरों से,
थोड़ा उनका घाव तो भरने दो।

तू खुद तेरा सबसे बड़ा सपना है,
छोटे सपनों के टूटने से निराश न हो,
तेरा सबसे बड़ा सपना तो अपने
आप में पूरा है।

शब्दों का पिंजरा

यहाँ शब्दों में बेचे जाते हैं जज़्बात,
अक्षरों के पिंजरों में कैद हैं एहसास।

एक बार खोल के देख उन पिंजरों को।
हर भावना को कहकर जताना पड़े तो वो भाव ही क्या?

कभी-कभी बिन कहे ही महसूस कर
दूसरों के दिल के हालात।

Hypocrites , hypocrites everywhere ,
All trying to hide behind dogmatic glare.

Now , it's time to destroy that fake layer,
sit back and reflect on the ideas they share.

मेरी ज़िंदगी, मेरा ख्वाब

एक ख्वाब देखा था मैंने,
जिसे पूरा करने में जिंदगी लगा दी।

अब जो पूरा हुआ तो अहसास हुआ,
ख्वाब की कीमत जिंदगी से अधिक आँक ली।

देश रंगीला

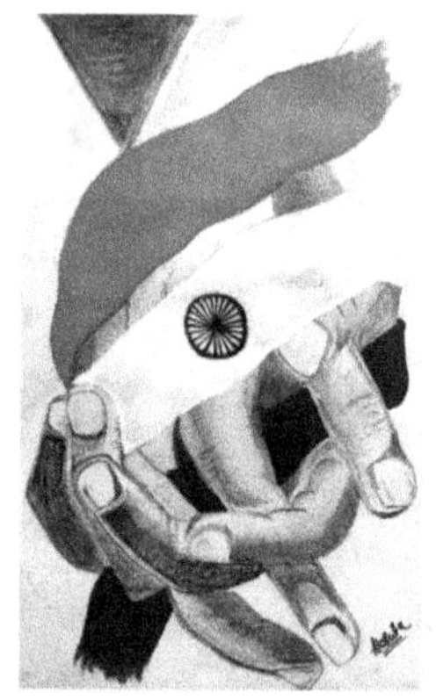

हर रंग में रंगा है ये मेरा देश,
मत छीन इसकी खूबसूरती,
पहनाकर इसे किसी एक रंग का वेश।

कहीं केसरी, कहीं हरा,
तो कहीं सफेद, कम-से-कम मत कर,
तिरंगे के इन रंगों में कोई भेद।

देश प्रेम

कितनी अजीब चीज है
न आज का 'देश प्रेम'!

देश की मिट्टी से है
पर उस पर रहने वाले लोगों से नहीं।

जाने कौन-सा कर्ज उतारना है मिट्टी का,
जिसमें लोगों की जान जाए तो भी सही।

मिट्टी के निर्जीव कणों को माथे पर लगाना है,
पर जिनमें जीवन है उनमें भेद करके,
जूतों के नीचे दबाना है।

अगर मिट्टी की इज्जत करते तो समझते,
मिट्टी को पानी चाहिए खून नहीं।

ABOUT THE AUTHOR

Sneha Abhishek (nee Tyagi) is presently teaching at Institute of Home Economics in University of Delhi. She has completed her Ph.D. (Education) from Jamia Millia Islamia. She is a trained Kathak dancer from Prayag Sangeet Samiti, Allahabad University.

She has won many accolades in dramatics. Through her first book as an author, she is also sharing her another skill of writing. Besides being a mother and home maker, she is always excited for new adventures.

In her own words...

> *"Today is not my day, In fact*
> *All days are mine*
> *I am the (s) hero of my filmy life*
> *Blessed being a woman"*

She would like to thank **Sangam Bawa** for providing illustrations.

–Sneha Abhishek

PLIGHT

The so called education of my life
Got struck in my throat as a knife.

Can not have the jobs that I want
Inspite of having degrees, I feel like an ant.

Whatever I do wherever I go
I hear the same and the answer is no.

Tears start rolling down on my cheek
To console myself I call them geek.

Education is now known as a revolutionary subject,
But for me it is still a stationary object.

Am telling you my very plight,
which shows that might is right.

All these words I want to save,
Cannot loose them in time's grave.

> *"Do you believe in Miracle?*
>
> *No!... It's alright*
>
> *Yes !... Then Understand this...*
>
> *Someone out there is CREATING*
> *the MIRACLE for YOU"*

मैंने जीना सीख लिया

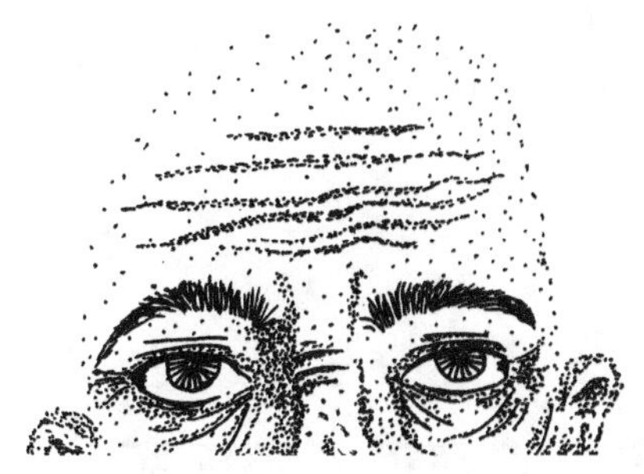

छोटी-छोटी बातों को भूल,
बड़ी बात को सीख लिया।

गिरते-पड़ते और लड़खड़ाते,
सीधा चलना सीख लिया।

क्या सही और क्या गलत,
अंतर ये समझना सीख लिया।

अपना पराया है कौन यहाँ,
सब एक ही है सीख लिया।

चुप रहूँ या बोल पड़ूँ,
प्रशन करना सीख लिया।

बहुत कुछ है अभी भी बाकी,
सीखने को जीवन में,
ये बात निरर्थक लगती है कि
मैंने जीना सीख लिया?

औरों की गलतियों से सीखते चलो,
तभी जी पाओगे;
पर उन्हें माफ भी करते चलो,
वरना नहीं जी पाओगे।

HAPPY BIRTHDAY
DARLING

Wishing an auspicious birthday to
My Bosom friend, My Husband,

My Best half, My life,
My Schoolmate, My Soulmate,

My Consort, My Guide,
My Partner in crime,

My Live in lover, My laughter,
My Advisor, My Funny Bone,
My Tranquilliser, My Strength,
My Shoulder to cry on,

My Pillow, My Alter ego,
My Engineer, My Sponsor,

My Cook, My mysterious Book,
My Sailor, My Sunshine,

My God's Gift, You are MINE,
Happy Birthday To You

तुम पर इस कदर मरते हैं कि
तुम्हारे बनाए खेल खेलते हैं,

हैं तो बादशाह हम ही, बस
जीतने तुम्हें देते हैं।

तुम नारी हो, बराबरी क्यों करती हो ?

तुम नारी हो, फिर बराबरी क्यों करती हो?
तुम अबला हो कमजोर हो जानती हो,
फिर बराबरी क्यों करती हो?

तुम मंदबुद्धि, चरित्रहीन हो,
फिर बराबरी क्यों करती हो?
तुम पुरुष नहीं हो न हो सकती हो,
फिर बराबरी क्यों करती हो?

शायद तुम खुदको अच्छे से जानती नहीं हो,
तभी तो पुरुष प्रधान समाज में होकर भी
बराबरी क्यों करती हो?

तुम नारी हो, फिर बराबरी क्यों करती हो?
अरी तुम सबला हो चरित्रवान हो चतुर हो,
फिर बराबरी क्यों करती हो?

तुम माँ हो, बेटी हो, बहन हो, बहू हो,
तुम जननी हो, अन्नपूर्णा हो,
तो बराबरी क्यों करती हो?

जब तुम ये सब जानती हो,
अपने अंदर की मर्दानगी को मानती हो,
तो फिर बराबरी क्यों करती हो?

हिचकिचाहट, आंसू, दर्द, डर,
अजीब सबको लगता है।

बात तो उसमें है जो इन सबके
बाद भी लगा रहता है।

ABOUT THE AUTHOR

Richa Srivastava is a 21 year-old budding writer, pursuing her graduation from university of Delhi. Inspired by the society around her which made her think about many issues which lead to her poems reflecting the image of society, she is on her way to achieve success in being a writer.

In her own words...

"Don't live in delusions
Life is meant to be yours and real"

She would like to thank **Mrigank Sharma** for providing illustrations.

–Richa Srivastava

समय

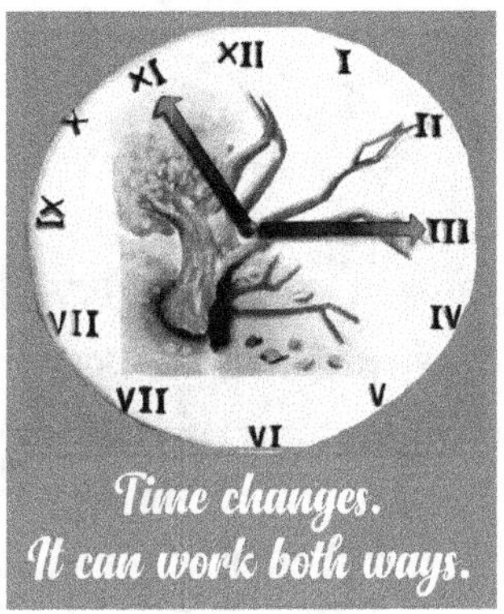

न ठहरा था,
न ठहरा हूँ,
मैं इतिहास का साथी।

साया हूँ,
मैं कल भी अटल था,
मैं आज भी अटल हूँ।

मैं समय हूँ,
हर घड़ी बदलता हूँ,

कल कुछ और था,
आज कुछ और हूँ।

हर इंसान मुझसे जुड़ा है,
जिसका मैं हुआ,
वो सितारों पे है,
और जिसका समय आया,
वो सितारा।

मैं आज भी हूँ,
मैं कल भी था।

जब जो हुआ उसका ज़िम्मेदार मैं हूँ,
जो होकर भी न हुआ,
उसका ज़िम्मेदार भी मैं ही हूँ।

मैं भला हूँ,
मैं बुरा भी,
मैं कैद हूँ,
इन घड़ी की सुइयों में।

मैं आज़ाद भी हूँ,
चलते रहने के लिए,
न ठहरा था, न ठहरा हूँ।

मैं इतिहास का साथी साया हूँ,
मैं कभी न रुकने वाला
समय हूँ।

YOLO

You only live once,
1 life and thousand rules,
Thousands to make you a fool.

1 life and many characters to Play,
Yet only 1 character to slay.

1 life and many goals to achieve,
1 goal with many obstacles to succeed.

1 life and many people to criticize,
Many people to low your voice.

1 life and many heartbeats to live,
1 heart and many heartbeats to skip.

Yolo!
You only Live once,
Don't waste it.

By just begin a part of grid,
Otherwise you will be in guilt.

Yolo!
You only Live once
Don't make your life worthless.

By just begin with stars,
Be a star and have fun with the maze.

Yolo!
You only Live once,
Don't hate it
by being a part of race,
Show them your grace.

Yolo!
Why to waste it
In counting stars and dates,
Let's enjoy the days.

Yolo!
Let's celebrate
The life we got,
Give your best shot,
Smile and shine.

Yolo!
To make a vow
From here and now,
To re-allow
To enjoy a new day with a wow.

PRONOUNS

Pronouns,
You and me,
Let's define us,
you, me and ourselves.

Let's define what we are,
Let's begin with her or she.

As the norms say,
"Ladies first."

The tantrum queen,
The princess of her house,
A homemaker and a baby sitter,
Pride of her house,
She is a goddess.

She is a mother,
yes she is a feminine.

Now let's define him or he,
A gentleman,
He is a masculine,
He is a savior,
He is a protector,
He is a Father.

He never cries,
He just smiles,
He flaunts his muscles.

Now let me introduce you to a new pronoun,
Which maybe not so profound,
They or them.

Who are they?
Are they adi-shakti?
Are they a curse?
Are they just a myth?

Or they are a shooting star,
Which may grant you a wish.

They are not our brother,
They are not our mother,
But yes they are humans,
They are homosexual,
But yes they are human,
They are humans,

They are you,
Just us,
You and me.

We ,
Let's not define people by their pronoun,
Let's just be a human,
 # pride,
#all pronouns matter.

ABOUT THE AUTHOR

Bipasha Bharti is currently pursuing her graduation in B.El.Ed at Institute of Home Economics in University of Delhi. She has been writing poems, prose and stories in English, Hindi and Roman Urdu since she was 8 years old.

Her hobbies include craft work, painting, sketching, cooking, baking, and practising make-up and hairstyles. She has received many awards and recognition in writing, painting, craft work and sketching during her school days. Through her first book as an author, she is sharing her skill of writing and illustrating with the world.

In her own words...

"If you want your life to change
You need to be ready for challenges
Embrace the striking waves ahead
Set out, let go, and breathe
Ride the wave of moment
Doing barrel rolls into your future"

"She has done all the illustrations for the poems in this book herself."

–Bipasha Bharti

FEELING LONELY

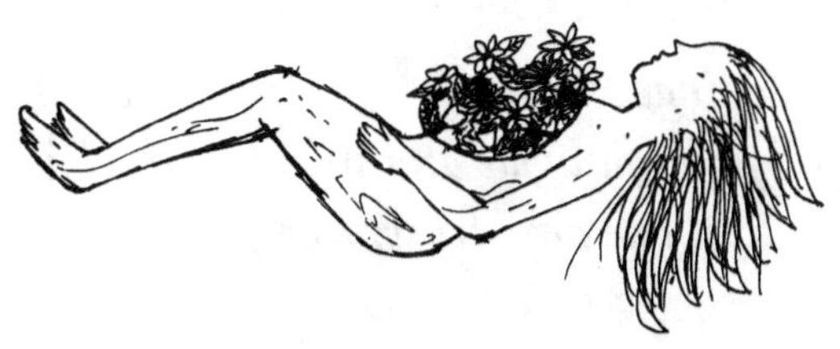

A few years ago,
I stepped Into a new phase of my life,
The senior school,
Having dreams and wishes, but,
Unfortunately, I was not knowing,
I will soon be trapped.

Fell into an incident or
I might call it as misunderstanding,
People stopped talking to me,
And, time flew, but I am there
Still, standing.

I was left alone, struggling
With that incident, surviving.

But, no one came by my side,
And, I was left depriving.

Years have gone by, I am still alone,
Left only with scars which hurt like stones,
My school life was only about
Studying or sitting beside a window.

Hoping, one day I will have a friend,
Who will know me and whom I will know,
But, one day, frustrated from this,
I took a decision.

I built my self-confidence,
and stood now brave,
I did not prove anyone that I was right,
And, the culprit was someone else,
But my head held high,
Face without fear and shy,
Eyes with bright shine,
And, heart with purity, did.

And, now, here, I stand,
Living my life happily,
With past forgotten,
And, with dreams and goals to achieve.

—Bipasha Bharti

सखी

सालों पहले बिछड़ गए थे जो दोस्त,
वो आज फिर मिले हैं,
बंजर हो गई थी जो जमीन,
आज वहाँ फिर नए फूल खिले हैं।

तू ना था तो,
तुझे याद कर रोते थे हम,
सोचते थे कब होगी यह दूरी कम।

याद करते थे वो लम्हे,

जो संग तेरे बिताए थे,

वो दिन जो हम ने

कभी साथ हँसकर,

तो कभी साथ रो के सजाए थे।

दिल में तुम ही हो,

बस जब से ज़िन्दगी में आए थे,

सच्चा साथी बस माना है तुम ही को,

तुम्हारी जगह किसी और को न दे पाएँगे।

लौट आने से तुम्हारे

ज़िन्दगी फिर हसीन लगती है,

बेरंग हो चुकी थी जो,

वो मेरी दुनिया फिर रंगीन लगती है।

आओ आज लग गले हम,

सारे ये फासले दूर कर दें,

बिछड़ न सकें दोबारा,

इस कदर एक दूजे को मजबूर कर दें।

बातें हैं ये वो जो मेरी माँ,

आप से कहना चाहती थी,

पर कह न पाती,

वही बातें मैं आपको बतला रही हूँ।

धन्यवाद करती हूँ आपका,
आपके आ जाने से
मेरी माँ के चेहरे पर लौट आई है,
वो खोई हुई मुस्कान,
इसलिए आज से मैं रहूँगी,
सदा आपकी मेहरबान।

–बिपाशा भारती

मौसम

बदलते वक्त के साथ बदल गया मौसम,
हौसले मत करो परस्त डटे रहो तुम।

आज पतझड़ है, कल वसंत आएगी,
यही उम्मीद नई उमंग लाएगी।

इन घने बादलों को देख,
भयभीत न हो तुम,
पैर तुम्हारे डगमगाते क्यों हैं?
निडर खड़े रहो तुम।

इस बदलते मौसम को देख
यही सोच रहे हो, अब क्या होगा?
इसी चिंता को छोड़,
तुम्हे सच का सामना करना होगा।

मौसम और वक़्त नहीं रहता एक सा,
आज गर्मी है तो कल बारिश आएगी,
सूख रही फसल फिर खिल जाएगी,
इसी तरह जीवन है हमारा,
कभी दुःख है तो कभी सुख,
पर यह देख बदलो न तुम ज़िन्दगी से रुख।

जीवन पल-पल बदलता है, समझती हूँ मैं,
तुम्हारा हृदय मचलता है,
पर इसी भय को तो तुम्हे,
अपनी हिम्मत बनाना है,
क्योंकि तुम्हे उन हर मुश्किल से जो लड़ना है।

रुकना नहीं है, बढ़ना है तुम्हे,
हर पल खुद को तैयार करना है तुम्हे,
इसलिए कहती हूँ,
खुद को कर बुलंद इतना,
हर मंज़िल तू पा सके,
उस मौसम रूपी जीवन की,
हर चुनौती को हरा सके।

यही चलता आया है यही चलेगा,
यह नियति का नियम है,
जो नहीं बदलेगा।

जीवन देता है कष्ट तुम्हे,
उस हर कष्ट को तुम सह जाओ।
इस तरह लड़ो तुम कि,
एक उदाहरण बन रह जाओ।

जिस दिन समझ लोगे
इस जीवन की ऋतुओं को,
उस दिन जान जाओगे
सफल हो चुके हो तुम,
उस राह में जो नहीं थी आसान।

उस दिन हाँ उस दिन,
लिखोगे तुम खुद की दास्तान।

-बिपाशा भारती

www.ingramcontent.com/pod-product-compliance
Lightning Source LLC
Chambersburg PA
CBHW050620160726
48003CB00003B/1267